#Follow

#FollowTheLeader

*A 100-Day Journey through the Life
of Jesus in 280 Characters or Less*

Rees J. Porcari

This publication is meant as a source of valuable information for the reader, however it is not meant as a substitute for direct expert assistance. If such level of assistance is required, the services of a competent professional should be sought.

ISBN: 978-1-6653-0508-2

⊗ This paper meets the requirements of ANSI/NISO Z39.48-1992 (Permanence of Paper)

103122

For the student who was as insecure as I was during those preteen and middle school years. I promise things will get better. Never forget that you are the pinnacle of God's creation, created in His image (Genesis 1:26–27). God looked over everything that He had made and knew that His creation needed you too. You are a wonderfully made creation (Psalm 139:13-14) that God made intentionally, with every aspect of you and your unique gifts in mind (Romans 12:6-8). Never let anyone tell you otherwise. And, finally, always remember you can do great things right now, and never let people tell you that you are too young (1 Timothy 4:12).

You can always use the word of God to dispel the lies of Satan.

"It is written: 'Man shall not live on bread alone, but on every word that comes from the mouth of God" (Matthew 4:4). . . . "It is also written: Do not put the Lord your God to the test" (Matthew 4:7). . . ."Away from me, Satan! For it is written, 'Worship the Lord your God, and serve him only.' Then the devil left him, and angels came and attended to him" (Matthew 4:10–11).

Going Forward: What lie do you need to squash?

_____

_____

_____

_____

_____

_____

_____

Don't hide what God is doing. Let your light shine loud and show others how great God is.

"You are the light of the world. A town built on a hill cannot be hidden" (Matthew 5:14). "In the same way let your light shine before others, that others may see your good deeds and glorify your father in heaven" (Matthew 5:16).

Going Forward: How can you use your light to show others about God?

_____

_____

_____

_____

_____

_____

_____

Don't do good to get the credit but because it is the right thing to do.

"Be careful not to practice your righteousness in front of others to be seen by them" (Matthew 6:1).

Going Forward: What good can you do that won't be seen?

_____

_____

_____

_____

_____

_____

_____

Possessions will waste away. Focus on what money cannot buy.

"But store up for yourselves treasures in heaven, where moths and vermin do not destroy and where thieves do not break in and steal. For where your treasure is, there your heart will be also" (Matthew 6:20–21).

Going Forward: What is most important in your life right now?

_____

_____

_____

_____

_____

_____

_____

Don't worry about things you cannot control because God has your back.

"Look at the birds of the air; they do not sow or reap or store away in barns, and yet your heavenly Father feeds them. Are you not much more valuable than they? Can any one of you by worrying add a single hour to your life?" (Matthew 6:26–27).

Going Forward: What are you worrying about that you can give to God?

_____

_____

_____

_____

_____

_____

_____

Having baggage or sin doesn't keep you from Jesus. It is why you need Jesus, and he wants you to come to him no matter how dirty you think you are.

"On hearing this, Jesus said, 'It is not the healthy who need a doctor, but the sick'" (Matthew 9:12). . . . "For I have not come to call the righteous, but sinners" (Matthew 9:13).

Going Forward: When was the last time you admitted you needed help? Is there something you need to ask for help with right now?

_____

_____

_____

_____

_____

_____

_____

Always stand up and defend those who are being bullied and those who cannot help themselves.

"When he (Jesus) saw the crowds, he had compassion on them, because they were harassed and helpless, like sheep without a shepherd" (Matthew 9:36).

Going Forward: What do you do when you see others being mistreated?

_____

_____

_____

_____

_____

_____

_____

Don't assume that someone else is doing it. If there is something that tugs on your heart, go and do it.

"Then he said to his disciples, 'The harvest is plentiful but the workers are few. Ask the Lord of the harvest, therefore, to send out workers into his harvest field.'" (Matthew 9:37–38).

Going Forward: What breaks your heart?

_____

_____

_____

_____

_____

_____

_____

You are so important to God that He knows how many hairs are on your head.

"And even the very hairs of your head are all numbered" (Matthew 10:30).

Going Forward: How does knowing how important you are change things?

_____

_____

_____

_____

_____

_____

_____

You can bring your burdens and worries daily to Jesus (even if they are the same ones), and he will always give you rest.

"Come to me, all you who are weary and burdened, and I will give you rest" (Matthew 11:28).

Going Forward: What burdens do you need to give to Jesus?

_____

_____

_____

_____

_____

_____

_____

People will recognize your character by your actions so show them something desirable.

"Make a tree good and its fruit will be good, or make a tree bad and its fruit will be bad, for a tree is recognized by its fruit" (Matthew 12:33).

Going Forward: What kind of fruit are you producing?

_____

_____

_____

_____

_____

_____

_____

When you are afraid, call out for help. Jesus will always be there to catch you.

"But when he saw the wind, he was afraid and, beginning to sink, cried out, "Lord, save me!" Immediately Jesus reached out his hand and caught him" (Matthew 14:30–31).

Going Forward: What can God help you with?

_____

_____

_____

_____

_____

_____

_____

Your words are powerful. Be careful how you use them.

"What goes into someone's mouth does not defile them, but what comes out of their mouth, that is what defiles them" (Matthew 15:11). . . . "But the things that come out of a person's mouth come from the heart, and those defile them" (Matthew 15:18).

Going Forward: How can you use your words to build? Do you need to repair a relationship where the wrong words were used?

_____

_____

_____

_____

_____

_____

_____

Jesus is not just at church, but wherever you gather together.

"For where two or three gather in my name, there am I with them" (Matthew 18:20).

Going Forward: Where do you feel Jesus most?

_____

_____

_____

_____

_____

_____

_____

You should always forgive those who wronged you—and yourself for past actions.

"Then Peter came to Jesus and asked, 'Lord how many times shall I forgive my brother and sister who sins against me? Up to seven times?' Jesus answered, 'I tell you, not seven times, but seventy-seven times.'" (Matthew 18:21–22).

Going Forward: Who do you need to forgive?

_____

_____

_____

_____

_____

_____

_____

Everyone who follows Jesus gets the same reward, and you shouldn't be mad but glad that God is so generous to all of us

"But he answered one of them, 'I am not being unfair to you, friend. Didn't you agree to work for a denarius? Take your pay and go. I want to give the who was hired last the same as I gave you. Don't I have the right to do what I want with my own money? Or are you envious because I am generous?'" (Matthew 20:13–15).

Going Forward: How do you feel when people who do less get the same as you?

_____

_____

_____

_____

_____

_____

_____

Do not use your authority for yourself but for the benefit of those you have been given authority over.

"Jesus called them together and said, "You know that the rulers of the Gentiles lord it over them, and their high officials exercise authority over them. Not so with you. Instead, whoever wants to become great among you must be your servant, and whoever wants to be first must be your slave—just as the Son of Man did not come to be served but to serve and to give his life as a ransom for many'" (Matthew 20:25–28).

Going Forward: How do you use your authority?

_____

_____

_____

_____

_____

_____

_____

Everyone is invited to the party of Jesus.

"So go to the street corners and invite to the banquet anyone you can find. So the servants went out into the streets and gathered all the people they could find, the bad as well as the good, and the wedding hall was filled with guests" (Matthew 22:9–10).

Going Forward: Who can you invite to the party?

_____

_____

_____

_____

_____

_____

_____

If you don't love others with God, then everything else will just fall to the ground.

"Jesus replied, 'Love the Lord your God with all your heart and with all your soul and with all of your mind.' This is the first and greatest commandment. And the second is like it: 'Love your neighbor as yourself. All the law and the prophets hang on these two commandments.'" (Matthew 22:37–40).

Going Forward: How can you love others better?

_____

_____

_____

_____

_____

_____

_____

When you show love toward others, you are showing love toward God.

"The King will reply, 'Truly I tell you, whatever you did for one of the least of these brothers and sisters of mine, you did for me.'" (Matthew 25:40).

Going Forward: Have you shown love to others who need it or just wish them well?

_____

_____

_____

_____

_____

_____

_____

Never use violence to defend Jesus.

"With that, one of Jesus's companions reached for his sword, drew it out, and struck the servant of the high priest, cutting off his ear. 'Put your sword back in its place,' Jesus said to him, 'for all who draw the sword will die by the sword'" (Matthew 26:51–52).

Going Forward: How do you defend Jesus?

_____

_____

_____

_____

_____

_____

_____

Don't just sit there. Tell the world about Jesus and everything you have learned from him and what he has done for you.

"Therefore go and make disciples of all nations, baptizing them in the name of the Father and of the Son and of the Holy Spirit, and teaching them to obey everything I have commanded you" (Matthew 28:19–20).

Going Forward: How can you tell others about Jesus? Write the names of some people you need to share Jesus with.

_____

_____

_____

_____

_____

_____

_____

Jesus will never leave you.

"And surely I am with you always, to the very end of the age" (Matthew 28:20).

Going Forward: Have you felt like Jesus is absent? Write how you felt and how he was there the whole time.

_____

_____

_____

_____

_____

_____

_____

If Jesus needed quiet time with God, so do you.

"Very early in the morning while it was still dark, Jesus got up, left the house, and went off to a solitary place, where he prayed" (Mark 1:35).

Going Forward: How do you take quiet time with Jesus?

_____

_____

_____

_____

_____

_____

_____

The only requirement to follow Jesus is to do just that. Follow.

"As he walked along, he saw Levi son of Alphaeus sitting at the tax collector's booth. 'Follow me,' Jesus told him, and Levi got up and followed him" (Mark 2:14).

Going Forward: Are/were you making it harder than it is for yourself or others to follow Jesus? Write about it here and how you can/did fix it.

_____

_____

_____

_____

_____

_____

_____

Don't get too busy. Rest is good and God created it just for you.

"Then he said to them, 'The Sabbath was made for man, not man for the Sabbath'" (Mark 2:27).

Going Forward: Are you getting enough rest? What do you do to get rest?

_____

_____

_____

_____

_____

_____

_____

Do what is right because it is right, even if it may get people angry or you in trouble.

"Some of them were looking for a reason to accuse Jesus, so they watched him closely to see if he would heal on the Sabbath. Jesus said to the man with the shriveled hand, 'Stand up in front of everyone.' Then Jesus asked them, 'Which is lawful on the Sabbath: to do good or to do evil, to save life or to kill?' But they remained silent. He looked at them in anger and, deeply distressed at their stubborn hearts, said to the man, 'Stretch out your hand.' He stretched it out and his hand was completely restored" (Mark 3:2–5).

Going Forward: How does considering what other people think affect your actions?

_____

_____

_____

_____

_____

_____

_____

You will experience rough times but Jesus will always be there to see you through them.

"A furious squall came up, and the waves broke over the boat, so that it was nearly swamped. Jesus was in the stern, sleeping on a cushion. The disciples woke him and said to him, 'Teacher, don't you care if we drown?' He got up, rebuked the wind and said to the waves, 'Quite! Be still!' Then the wind died down and it was completely calm" (Mark 4:37–39).

Going Forward: How do you lean on Jesus?

_____

_____

_____

_____

_____

_____

_____

Your story matters, and God will use it to do great things, so share it with others.

"'Go home to your own people and tell them how much the Lord has done for you, and how he has had mercy on you.' So the man went away and began to tell in the Decapolis how much Jesus had done for him. And all the people were amazed" (Mark 5:19–20).

Going Forward: How can you share your story with others? What parts matter most?

_____

_____

_____

_____

_____

_____

_____

In everything that you do for Jesus, never forget his desire to refresh and give you rest.

"The apostles gathered around Jesus and reported to him all they had done and taught. Then, because so many people were coming and going that they did not even have a chance to eat, he said to them, 'Come with me by yourselves to a quiet place and get some rest'" (Mark 6:30–31).

Going Forward: How do you spend time with Jesus and let him give you rest?

_____

_____

_____

_____

_____

_____

_____

If it hurts someone made in God's image, it is against God.

"Thus you nullify the word of God by your tradition that you have handed down. And you do many things like that" (Mark 7:13).

Going Forward: Discuss if you have treated someone (or treated yourself) in a way that hurts.

_____

_____

_____

_____

_____

_____

_____

You will have to give up some things to follow Jesus, but it will be worth it in the end.

"Then he called the crowd to him along with his disciples and said: 'Whoever wants to be my disciple must deny themselves and take up their cross and follow me. For whoever wants to save their life will lose it, but whoever loses their life for me and for the gospel will save it'" (Mark 8:34–36).

Going Forward: What habit do you need to give up for God?

_____

_____

_____

_____

_____

_____

_____

Don't be afraid of unbelief. Jesus will not get mad but will help.

"'Everything is possible for one who believes.' Immediately the boy's father exclaimed, 'I do believe; help me overcome my unbelief!'" (Mark 9:23–24). . . . "The boy looked so much like a corpse that many said, 'He's dead.' But Jesus took him by the hand and lifted him to his feet, and he stood up'" (Mark 9:26–27).

Going Forward: Write down any doubts you have and ask Jesus to help you overcome them.

_____

_____

_____

_____

_____

_____

_____

Followers of Jesus come in different forms with different beliefs, but we are all on the same team.

"'Do not stop him,' Jesus said. 'For no one who does a miracle in my name can in the next moment say anything bad about me, for whoever is not against us is for us'" (Mark 9:39–40).

Going Forward: How do you view other Christians outside your church?

_____

_____

_____

_____

_____

_____

_____

If Jesus was obedient to his parents, we should be too.

"Then he went down to Nazareth with them and was obedient to them" (Luke 2:51).

Going Forward: How can you honor your parents more?

_____

_____

_____

_____

_____

_____

_____

Jesus didn't start his ministry until the time was right. Your time will come too, just be patient with God's timing.

"Now Jesus himself was about thirty years old when he began his ministry" (Luke 3:23).

Going Forward: Is there something you are trying to make happen before it is time?

_____

_____

_____

_____

_____

_____

_____

Even if life takes you to the edge of a cliff, Jesus will always be able to walk you back to safety.

"They got up, drove him out of the town, and took him to the brow of the hill on which the town was built, in order to throw him off the cliff. But he walked right through the crowd and went on his way" (Luke 4:29–30).

Going Forward: How can Jesus help you when the cliff is coming?

_____

_____

_____

_____

_____

_____

_____

Moving can be difficult and you and others may not want it, but it is an opportunity to proclaim the kingdom to many more people.

"At daybreak, Jesus went out to a solitary place. The people were looking for him and when they came to where he was, they tried to keep him from leaving them. But he said, 'I must proclaim the good news of the kingdom of God to the other towns also, because that is why I was sent'" (Luke 4:42–43).

Going Forward: How can you expand your circle?

_____

_____

_____

_____

_____

_____

_____

Sins and mistakes don't disqualify you from Jesus, but are why you need him.

"But the Pharisees and the teachers of the law who belonged to their sect complained to his disciples, 'Why do you eat and drink with tax collectors and sinners?' Jesus answered them, 'It is not the healthy who need a doctor, but the sick. I have not come to call the righteous, but sinners to repentance'" (Luke 5:30-32).

Going Forward: Who do you need to invite to the table of Jesus to taste the grace?

_____

_____

_____

_____

_____

_____

_____

A close, small circle of friends is better than just hanging out with a crowd.

"When morning came, he called his disciples to him and chose twelve of them, whom he also designated apostles" (Luke 6:13).

Going Forward: Do you care about the quality or quantity of friends? Write about it here.

_____

_____

_____

_____

_____

_____

_____

When you do a favor or help someone, don't keep track and expect to be paid back. Do it out of love.

"And if you lend to those from whom you expect repayment, what credit is that to you? Even sinners lend to sinners, expecting to be repaid in full" (Luke 6:34).

Going Forward: Why do you help people?

_____

_____

_____

_____

_____

_____

_____

We all have our faults. We need to look at ourselves before we think about other people's faults.

"How can you say to your brother, 'Brother, let me take the speck out of your eye,' when you yourself fail to see the plank in your own eye? You hypocrite, first take the plank out of your eye, and then you will see clearly to remove the speck from your brother's eye" (Luke 6:42).

Going Forward: What do you need to fix in yourself?

_____

_____

_____

_____

_____

_____

_____

Building a solid foundation protects you from the storms of life.

"They are like a man building a house, who dug down deep and laid the foundation on rock. When a flood came, the torrent struck that house but could not shake it, because it was well built. But the one who hears my words and does not put them into practice is like a man who built a house on the ground without a foundation. The moment the torrent struck that house, it collapsed and its destruction was complete" (Luke 6:48–49).

Going Forward: How can you have a foundation of stone?

_____

_____

_____

_____

_____

_____

_____

Don't hide your light. Throw it up and let it shine for all to see.

"No one lights a lamp and hides it in a clay jar or puts it under a bed. Instead, they put it on a stand, so that those who come in can see the light" (Luke 8:16).

Going Forward: How can your light shine at its brightest?

_____

_____

_____

_____

_____

_____

_____

Children are important to God and never let some-one tell you otherwise.

"Whoever welcomes this little child in my name welcomes me; and whoever welcomes me welcomes the one who sent me. For it is the one who is least among you all who is the greatest" (Luke 9:48).

Going Forward: How do you see your value?

_____

_____

_____

_____

_____

_____

_____

Don't assume someone else will do the work—people like you are fewer than you think.

"He told them, 'The harvest is plentiful, but the workers are few. Ask the Lord of the harvest, therefore, to send out workers into his harvest field'" (Luke 10:2).

Going Forward: What do you see that needs to be done?

_____

_____

_____

_____

_____

_____

_____

Things you do for Jesus are good, but never let them replace the fact heaven knows your name.

"However, do not rejoice that the spirits submit to you, but rejoice that your names are written in heaven" (Luke 10:20).

Going Forward: How do you view your relationship with God?

_____

_____

_____

_____

_____

_____

_____

Everyone is your neighbor. Help and have mercy on all.

"'Which of these three do you think was a neighbor to the man who fell into the hands of robbers?' The expert in the law replied, 'The one who had mercy on him.' Jesus told him, 'Go and do likewise'" (Luke 10:36–37).

Going Forward: Do you treat all people the same? How can you change that if not?

_____

_____

_____

_____

_____

_____

_____

Be careful at the things you look at. Images are more dangerous than you know and can affect everything about you.

"Your eye is the lamp of the body. When your eyes are healthy, your whole body also is full of light. But when they are unhealthy your body is also full of darkness. See to it, then, that the light within you is not darkness" (Luke 11:34–35).

Going Forward: Is there something you need to stop looking at? Who can help you with this?

_____

_____

_____

_____

_____

_____

_____

Do not do things just to get recognition and good seats.

"Woe to you Pharisees, because you love the most important seats in the synagogues and respectful greetings in the marketplace" (Luke 11:43).

Going Forward: Do you do good for praise or for love?

_____

_____

_____

_____

_____

_____

_____

Don't hurt people with your knowledge but use it for their benefit to help them.

"Jesus replied, 'And you experts in the law, woe to you, because you load people down with burdens they can hardly carry, and you yourselves will not lift one finger to help them'" (Luke 11:46).

Going Forward: How do you use your knowledge? How do you make people feel when you share your knowledge?

_____

_____

_____

_____

_____

_____

_____

Secrets will always come to the surface. Better to find someone to share them with.

"There is nothing concealed that will not be disclosed, or hidden that will not be made known. What you have said in the dark will be heard in the daylight, and what you have whispered in the ear in the inner rooms will be proclaimed from the roofs" (Luke 12:2–3).

Going Forward: Is there something you need to confess to someone you trust? Write about it here and start by letting God know.

_____

_____

_____

_____

_____

_____

_____

Worrying doesn't change anything so don't let it bother you.

"Who of you by worrying can add a single hour to your life? Since you cannot do this very little thing, why do you worry about the rest?" (Luke 12:25–26).

Going Forward: Is there a worry you need to give to Jesus? Write about it here.

_____

_____

_____

_____

_____

_____

_____

Make peace with your enemies because they can drag you down with them.

"As you are going with your adversary to the magistrate, try hard to be reconciled on the way, or your adversary may drag you off to the judge, and the judge turn you over to the officer, and the officer throw you into prison. I tell you, you will not get out until you have paid the last penny" (Luke 12:58–59).

Going Forward: Who do you need to forgive? (This can be you too.)

_____

_____

_____

_____

_____

_____

_____

Never let rules get in the way of helping people. People are more important. Always.

"The Lord answered him, 'You hypocrites! Doesn't each of you on the Sabbath untie your ox or donkey from the stall and lead it out to give it water? Then should not this woman, a daughter of Abraham, whom Satan has kept bound for eighteen long years, be set free on the Sabbath day from what bound her?'" (Luke 13:15–16).

Going Forward: Are people or rules more important to you?

_____

_____

_____

_____

_____

_____

_____

If you do not plan ahead, it will not work out.

"Suppose one of you wants to build a tower. Won't you first sit down and estimate the cost to see if you have enough money to complete it? For if you lay the foundation and are not able to finish it, everyone who sees it will ridicule you, saying, 'This person began to build and wasn't able to finish.'" (Luke 14:28–30).

Going Forward: What is your plan for your goals?

_____

_____

_____

_____

_____

_____

_____

When someone comes to God, there is a party in heaven, so act like it down here.

"I tell you that in the same way there will be more rejoicing in heaven over one sinner who repents than over ninety-nine righteous persons who do not need to repent" (Luke 15:7).

Going Forward: How do you react when someone (or you) accepts Jesus?

_____

_____

_____

_____

_____

_____

_____

When someone comes to God, He (God) wants to tell everyone about it. We should act the same way.

"And when she finds it, she calls her friends and neighbors and says, 'Rejoice with me; I have found my lost coin.' In the same way, I tell you, there is rejoicing in the presence of the angels of God over one sinner who repents" (Luke 15:9–10).

Going Forward: How do you tell people about yourself and others who have come to God?

_____

_____

_____

_____

_____

_____

_____

You are never too far from the Father, and when you turn to Him, He runs toward you, His child.

"So he got up and went to his father. 'But while he was still a long way off, his father saw him and was filled with compassion for him; he ran to his son, threw his arms around him, and kissed him'" (Luke 15:20).

Going Forward: Do you need to turn around? Do you know someone else who you can help know this truth?

_____

_____

_____

_____

_____

_____

_____

Your status with the Father is not based on your work, but because you are his child.

"But he answered his father, 'Look! All these years I've been slaving for you and never disobeyed your orders. Yet you never gave me even a young goat so I could celebrate with my friends. But when this son of yours who has squandered your property with prostitutes comes home, you kill the fattened calf for him!' 'My son,' the father said, 'you are always with me, and everything I have is yours'" (Luke 15:29–31).

Going Forward: What do you think makes the Father love you? What about others?

_____

_____

_____

_____

_____

_____

_____

If someone apologizes, you need to accept it no matter what the wrong.

"If your brother or sister sins against you, rebuke them, and if they repent, forgive them" (Luke 17:3).

Going Forward: Is there someone that you are withholding forgiveness from? (This can be yourself too.)

_____

_____

_____

_____

_____

_____

_____

When God does something for you, always remember to give him thanks and praise.

"Jesus asked, 'Were not all ten cleansed? Where are the other nine? Has no one returned to give praise to God except this foreigner?' Then he said to him, 'Rise and go; your faith has made you well'" (Luke 17:17–19).

Going Forward: When was the last time you thanked God for something? Write about it here.

_____

_____

_____

_____

_____

_____

_____

Never give up praying. In time, God will answer.

"And will not God bring about justice for his chosen ones, who cry out to him day and night? Will he keep putting them off? I tell you, he will see that they get justice, and quickly" (Luke 18:7–8).

Going Forward: Is there a prayer you stopped because you think God didn't care? Write about it here.

_____

_____

_____

_____

_____

_____

_____

Your "good deeds" do not put you in a higher position with God.

"The Pharisee stood by himself and prayed: 'God, I thank you that I am not like other people—robbers, evildoers, adulterers—or even like this tax collector. I fast twice a week and give a tenth of all I get.' But the tax collector stood at a distance. He would not even look up to heaven, but beat his breast and said, 'God, have mercy on me, a sinner.' I tell you that this man, rather than the other, went home justified before God. For all those who exalt themselves will be humbled, and those who humble themselves will be exalted" (Luke 18:11–14).

Going Forward: Which above are you?

_____

_____

_____

_____

_____

_____

_____

The things you give up to follow Jesus will be nothing compared to what you will receive.

"'Truly I tell you,' Jesus said to them, 'no one who has left home or wife or brothers or sisters or parents or children for the sake of the kingdom of God will fail to receive many times as much in this age, and in the age to come eternal life'" (Luke 18:29–30).

Going Forward: Is there something you are afraid to give up for Jesus?

_____

_____

_____

_____

_____

_____

_____

It is not about what you have been given but what you do with what you have been given.

"His master replied, 'I will judge you by your own words, you wicked servant! You knew, did you, that I am a hard man, taking out what I did not put in, and reaping what I did not sow? Why then didn't you put my money on deposit, so that when I came back, I could have collected it with interest?'" (Luke 19:22–23).

Going Forward: How are you using the skills that God gave you?

_____

_____

_____

_____

_____

_____

_____

Jesus's reaction to the sins of others was sorrow, and ours should be too.

"As he approached Jerusalem and saw the city, he wept over it and said, 'If you, even you, had only known on this day what would bring you peace—but now it is hidden from your eyes'" (Luke 19:41–42).

Going Forward: How do you react to the sin of others? What about your sin?

_____

_____

_____

_____

_____

_____

_____

Remember who Jesus is. If it doesn't sound like him 100 percent of the time, it is 100 percent not him.

"He replied: 'Watch out that you are not deceived. For many will come in my name, claiming, "I am he," and, "The time is near." Do not follow them'" (Luke 21:8).

Going Forward: Is there a false Jesus you need to turn away from?

_____

_____

_____

_____

_____

_____

_____

We will all be faced with temptation, but God is here to help us resist it.

"On reaching the place, he said to them, 'Pray that you will not fall into temptation'" (Luke 22:40).

Going Forward: How do you deal with temptation?

_____

_____

_____

_____

_____

_____

_____

Stay strong and shine bright. Bad will never over-come your good.

"The light shines in the darkness and the darkness has not overcome it" (John 1:5).

Going Forward: Do you ever feel your good is going nowhere? What can you do to change this?

_____

_____

_____

_____

_____

_____

_____

Don't be so busy that you miss the miracle.

"And the master of the banquet tasted the water that had been turned into wine. He did not realize where it had come from, though the servants who had drawn the water knew" (John 2:9).

Going Forward: How are you taking the time to see what is happening around you?

_____

_____

_____

_____

_____

_____

_____

God sent Jesus for YOU, and no matter what you have done or will do, he will save YOU if you believe in Him.

"For God so loved the world that he gave his one and only Son, that whoever believes in him shall not perish but have eternal life. For God did not send his Son into the world to condemn the world, but to save the world through him" (John 3:16–17).

Going Forward: Have you ever replaced "the world" with your name? What about the name of a person who is not kind or has hurt you? How does that change things?

_____

_____

_____

_____

_____

_____

_____

Jesus knows that everyone is equal and no one is off limits.

"When a Samaritan woman came to draw water, Jesus said to her, 'Will you give me a drink?' (His disciples had gone into the town to buy food.) The Samaritan woman said to him, 'You are a Jew and I am a Samaritan woman. How can you ask me for a drink?' (For Jews do not associate with Samaritans.)" (John 4:7–9).

Going Forward: How do you treat people your crowd thinks less of? Do you need to change the attitude of yourself or others?

_____

_____

_____

_____

_____

_____

_____

Jesus knows everything we ever do but desires us anyway, and we need to tell everyone about that good news.

"Then, leaving her water jar, the woman went back to the town and said to the people, 'Come, see a man who told me everything that I ever did'" (John 4:28–29).

Going Forward: When was the last time you told people about how much Jesus cares, even when we do wrong?

Reading the Bible is good, but if that is all you do it will get you nowhere.

"You study the Scriptures diligently because you think that in them you have eternal life. These are the very Scriptures that testify about me, yet you refuse to come to me to have life" (John 5:39–40).

Going Forward: How can you put the words of Jesus into action?

_____

_____

_____

_____

_____

_____

_____

Jesus will use whatever you have to do amazing things (no matter how small).

"'Here is a boy with five small barley loaves and two small fish, but how far will they go among so many?' Jesus said, 'Have the people sit down.' There was plenty of grass in that place, and they sat down (about five thousand men were there). Jesus then took the loaves, gave thanks, and distributed to those who were seated as much as they wanted. He did the same with the fish" (John 6:9–11).

Going Forward: Do you think you don't have enough to make a difference? How can you change that mindset?

_____

_____

_____

_____

_____

_____

_____

You belong to Jesus and there is nothing you can do to lose or earn his love.

"And this is the will of him who sent me, that I shall lose none of all those he has given me, but raise them up at the last day. For my Father's will is that everyone who looks at the Son and believes in him shall have eternal life, and I will raise them up at the last day" (John 6:39–40).

Going Forward: Have you felt the love of Jesus is dependent on you? How can you change that?

_____

_____

_____

_____

_____

_____

_____

You need to look beyond what you can see.

"Stop judging by mere appearances, but instead judge correctly" (John 7:24).

Going Forward: How do you judge people?

_____

_____

_____

_____

_____

_____

_____

Anyone who wants Jesus is invited. Let's make sure everyone knows it in our loudest voice.

"On the last and greatest day of the festival, Jesus stood and said in a loud voice, 'Let anyone who is thirsty come to me and drink'" (John 7:37).

Going Forward: How are you inviting others to Jesus?

_____

_____

_____

_____

_____

_____

_____

Even in the worst of times, Jesus will always be with you to give you light and life.

"When Jesus spoke again to the people, he said, 'I am the light of the world. Whoever follows me will never walk in darkness, but will have the light of life'" (John 8:12).

Going Forward: How can you remember to follow Jesus when life gets messy?

_____

_____

_____

_____

_____

_____

_____

Jesus can rescue you from the control of sin and make you a permanent member of his family.

"Jesus replied, 'Very truly I tell you, everyone who sins is a slave to sin. Now a slave has no permanent place in the family, but a son belongs to it forever. So if the Son sets you free, you will be free indeed'" (John 8:34–36).

Going Forward: Have you asked Jesus to set you free? What is keeping you from that if not?

_____

_____

_____

_____

_____

_____

_____

Bad things will happen that are not because you did something, but because God is going to do something through you.

"As he went along, he saw a man blind from birth. His disciples asked him, 'Rabbi, who sinned, this man or his parents, that he was born blind?' 'Neither this man nor his parents sinned,' said Jesus, 'but this happened so that the works of God might be displayed in him'" (John 9:1–3).

Going Forward: How can you react better the next time something bad happens?

_____

_____

_____

_____

_____

_____

_____

Jesus will always go before you . . . all you need to do is follow and you will be okay.

"When he has brought out all his own, he goes ahead of them, and his sheep follow him because they know his voice" (John 10:4).

Going Forward: Do you trust Jesus enough to just follow? How can you make it easier?

_____

_____

_____

_____

_____

_____

_____

Jesus has come not just to give you life but to give you the best life.

"I have come that they may have life, and have it to the full" (John 10:10).

Going Forward: How has your life or the life of someone you know gotten better by following Jesus?

_____

_____

_____

_____

_____

_____

_____

Jesus cried and it is okay for us to as well.

"Jesus wept" (John 11:35).

Going Forward: How do you feel about crying? When was the last time something made you cry and what was it?

_____

_____

_____

_____

_____

_____

_____

If Jesus came to save us, we should never threaten people with his judgment because that is not why he came.

"For I did not come to judge the world, but to save the world" (John 12:47).

Going Forward: How do you use the name of Jesus?

_____

_____

_____

_____

_____

_____

_____

It is not how often you read the Bible, your church attendance, or anything else. People should be able to know you follow Jesus by how you treat others.

"A new command I give you: Love one another. As I have loved you, so you must love one another. By this everyone will know you are my disciples, if you love one another" (John 13:34–35).

Going Forward: How do people know you are a Jesus follower? Do the reasons need to change?

God's house is big. There are rooms for me and you and many, many others. Let's fill the house.

"My Father's house has many rooms; if that were not so, would I have told you that I am going there to prepare a place for you?" (John 14:2).

Going Forward: How are you helping to fill the house?

_____

_____

_____

_____

_____

_____

_____

With Jesus, you can let your worry disappear.

"Peace I leave with you; my peace I give you. I do not give to you as the world gives. Do not let your hearts be troubled and do not be afraid" (John 14:27).

Going Forward: What is a worry you need to give to Jesus?

_____

_____

_____

_____

_____

_____

_____

Pruning will hurt at the time, but you will come back better than ever.

"Every branch that does bear fruit he (the Father) prunes so that it will be even more fruitful" (John 15:2).

Going Forward: Are there things that are hard right now and don't make sense? How can you remember that this is part of the process sometimes? Is there someone you can talk to about it?

_____

_____

_____

_____

_____

_____

_____

Stick with Jesus and he will stick with you.

"I am the vine; you are the branches. If you remain in me and I in you, you will bear much fruit; apart from me you can do nothing" (John 15:5).

Going Forward: How can you always stick with Jesus? Can someone help you do this?

_____

_____

_____

_____

_____

_____

_____

A command is not a suggestion. The number one for Jesus is to love others with no strings attached, just like he did for us.

"My command is this: Love each other as I have loved you" (John 15:12).

Going Forward: How can you obey this command?

_____

_____

_____

_____

_____

_____

_____

Following Jesus is an invitation into a relationship, and he lets you know everything he knows.

"You are my friends if you do what I command. I no longer call you servants, because a servant does not know his master's business. Instead, I have called you friends, for everything I have learned from my Father I have made known to you" (John 15:15).

Going Forward: How does it feel to know Jesus calls you friend? Does this change anything for you?

_____

_____

_____

_____

_____

_____

_____

If he mentioned loving one another two times in five verses, it must be pretty important.

"This is my command: Love one another" (John 15:17).

Going Forward: How can you take this command as seriously as Jesus wants us to?

_____

_____

_____

_____

_____

_____

_____

In life, bad and sad things will happen, but Jesus is always greater.

"I have told you these things, so that in me you may have peace. In this world you will have trouble. But take heart! I have overcome the world" (John 16:33).

Going Forward: How does it make you feel that bad things will still happen to you as you follow Jesus? Is there someone you have seen walk through bad things well?

_____

_____

_____

_____

_____

_____

_____

Jesus not only has been praying for you long before you were born but wants all of us to have the same connectedness that he has with the Father.

"My prayer is not for them alone. I pray also for those who will believe in me through their message, that all of them may be one, Father, just as you are in me and I am in you" (John 17:20–21).

Going Forward: How does it make you feel that Jesus prayed for you? How does this change your view of yourself and others?

Jesus has sent us on a mission just like he was on, so we need to act as he did.

"Again, Jesus said, 'Peace be with you! As the Father has sent me, I am sending you'" (John 20:21).

Going Forward: What is your mission field?

_____

_____

_____

_____

_____

_____

_____

Even from the first days after the resurrection, Jesus was thinking about you believing in him, and he called you blessed.

"Then Jesus told him, 'Because you have seen me, you have believed; blessed are those who have not seen and yet believed'" (John 20:29).

Going Forward: How does it feel that Jesus called you blessed? What does this mean for others?

_____

_____

_____

_____

_____

_____

_____

Jesus has his plans just for you, so don't worry about what his plans for others are.

"When Peter saw him, he asked, 'Lord, what about him?' Jesus answered, 'If I want him to remain alive until I return, what is that to you? You must follow me'" (John 21:21–22).

Going Forward: How can you stay focused on what Jesus has for you?

_____

_____

_____

_____

_____

_____

_____

Some stay local. Some go far. Whichever path is for you, the Holy Spirit will provide just what you need.

"But you will receive power when Holy Spirit comes on you; and you will be my witnesses in Jerusalem, and in all Judea and Samaria, and to the ends of the earth" (Acts 1:8).

Going Forward: Where is your mission field and what abilities have the Holy Spirit given you to accomplish your goals?

_____

_____

_____

_____

_____

_____

_____

About the Author

Rees lives in North Georgia and has been leading children and students for ten years combined. He has a bachelor's from Clemson University and a master's from Dallas Theological Seminary.

You can connect with Rees on Twitter and Instagram @ReesPorcari.

For more content, you can follow along on Twitter @TheBibleTweeted or on Instagram @MicroDevotionals.

9 781665 305082